Amazing Whales

Jillian Powell

RIGBY

Contents

What Are Whales?

Whales are the biggest animals in the sea. They look like fish, but they are not fish. Whales are **mammals**. Read this book to find out more about the amazing life of whales.

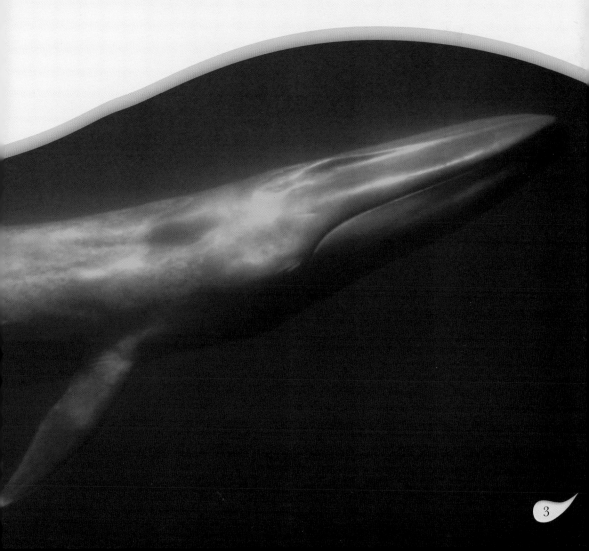

There are two kinds of whales. There are toothed whales and **baleen** whales. Most whales are toothed whales.

Whales

Toothed Whales

- Beluga whale
- Dolphin
- Killer whale
- Pilot whale
- Sperm whale

Baleen Whales

- Blue whale
- Finback whale
- Grey whale
- Humpback whale
- Right whale

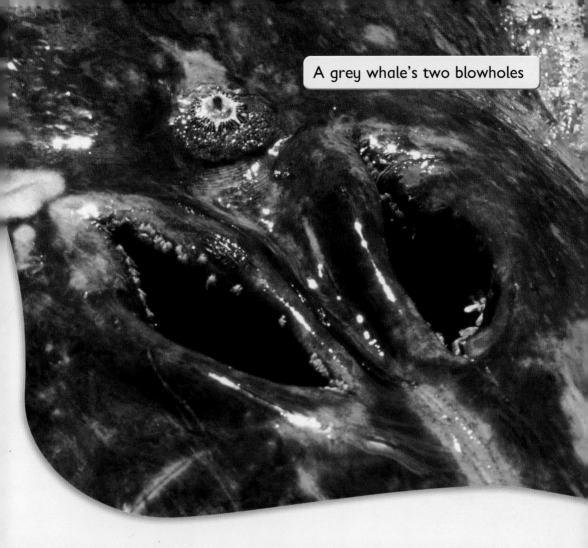

A grey whale's two blowholes

All whales have a **blowhole** on top of their head. They breathe through the hole. The hole is open when the whales breathe. It is closed when the whales are under the water.

Toothed whales have one blowhole. Baleen whales have two holes for breathing.

Toothed whales have teeth. They use their teeth to catch small fish and other sea animals. Dolphins and beluga whales are toothed whales.

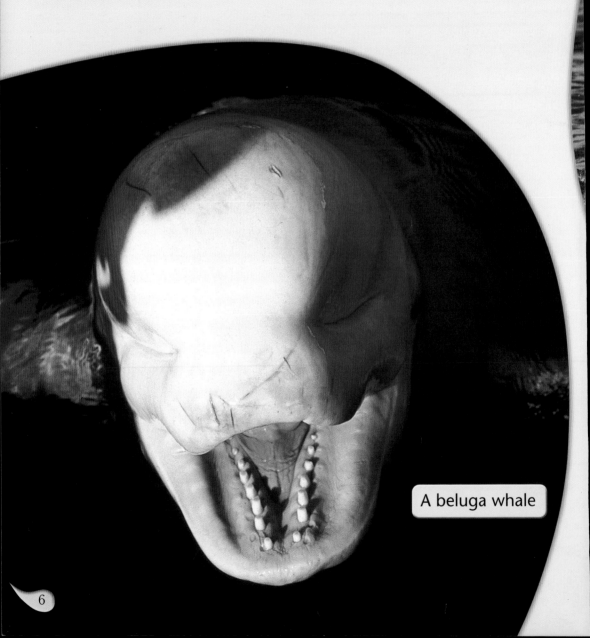

A beluga whale

A grey whale

baleen

Baleen whales do not have teeth. They have a
baleen. A baleen looks like a comb. Right whales
and grey whales are baleen whales.

A Whale's Life

Like all mammals, whales give birth to live babies. A baby whale is called a **calf**. A female whale can have a calf every one to three years.

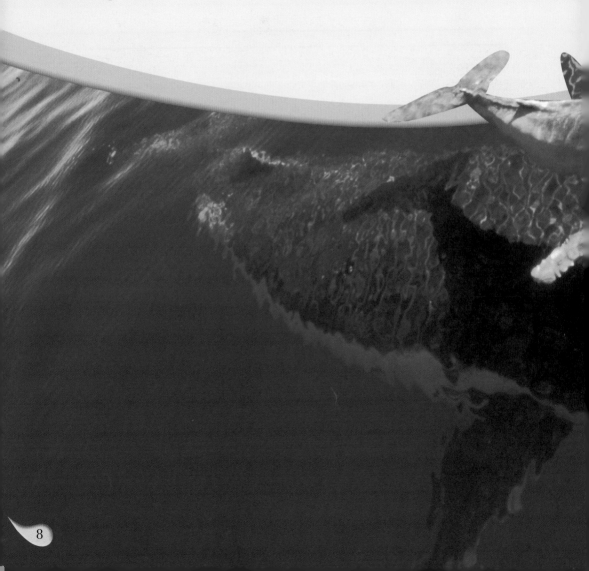

A calf can swim as soon as it is born. It lives with its mother for a year or more. The calf needs to drink its mother's milk.

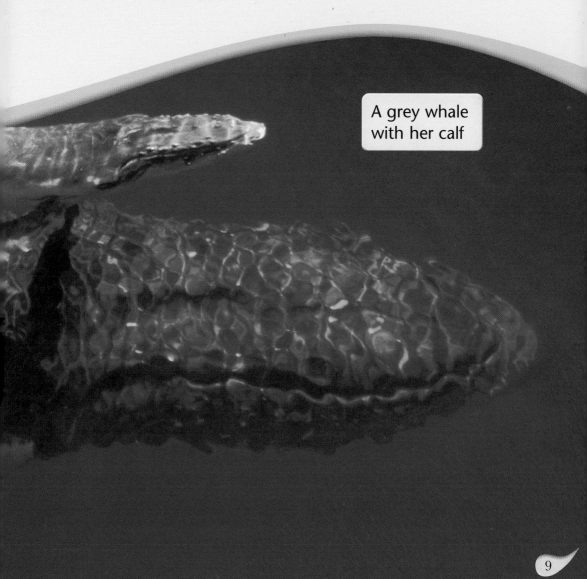

A grey whale with her calf

Toothed whales eat fish and other sea animals. Baleen whales eat lots of tiny living things such as small fish, shellfish and sea animals. Some baleen whales can eat 40 million tiny sea animals in one day!

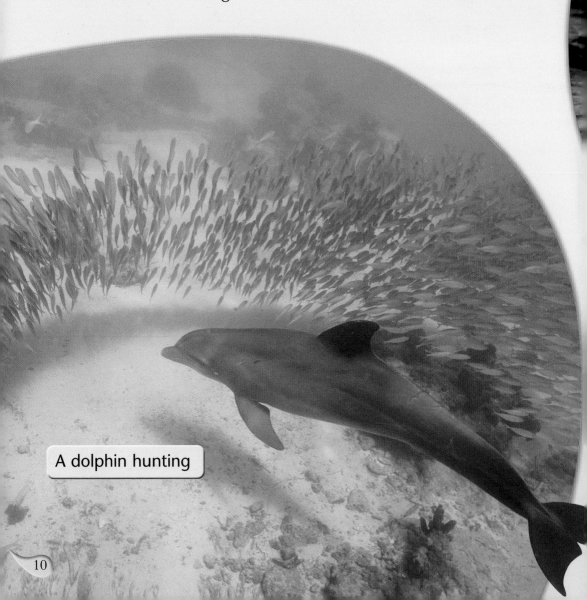

A dolphin hunting

A right whale feeding

Most baleen whales swim with their mouth open. They let water and living things into their open mouth. Then they close their mouth and push the water out. They eat the living things trapped in their baleen.

All whales move their tail up and down to swim under the water. They use their **flippers** to turn their body. Whales use their flippers and tail to stop too.

Humpback whales swimming

A pod of beluga whales

A group of whales that live together is called a **pod**. Baleen whales swim in small pods or alone. Toothed whales swim in large pods.

All whales make sounds under the water. They do this to talk to each other. Some whales sound as if they are singing. Blue whales sing the loudest. Their singing is louder than a jumbo jet!

A whale's song being recorded

A dolphin with its catch

Toothed whales make sounds to find sea animals to eat. The sounds bounce off animals in the sea. Each sound comes back to the whale. It tells the whale where an animal is, how big it is and how fast it is swimming.

People trying to help a whale stuck on a beach

In the past, people hunted whales for their meat, fat and oil. Today, most whale hunting has been stopped. But some people still hunt whales.

Other whales die because they get
trapped in fishing nets, or because
they get stuck on beaches.

Amazing Whales

The blue whale is the biggest whale. A blue whale can grow to be 30 metres long. That's as long as three buses!

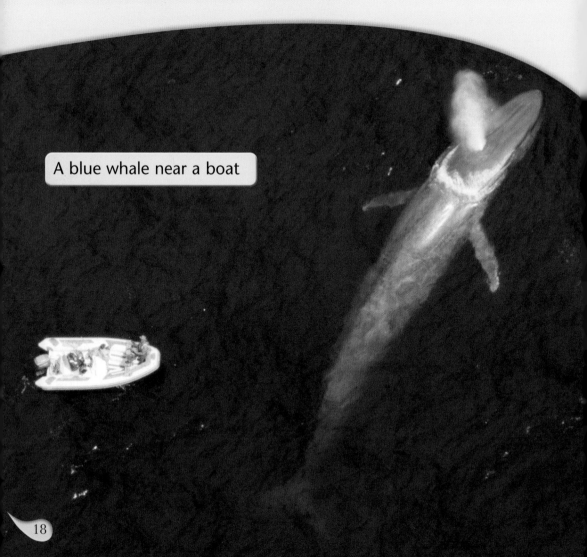

A blue whale near a boat

A dwarf sperm whale

The dwarf sperm whale is the smallest whale. A dwarf sperm whale grows under three metres long. That's as long as a small car.

Killer whales and pilot whales are the fastest whales. They can swim up to 30 miles per hour. They swim fast when they are hunting food to eat.

A pilot whale

A killer whale

The deadliest whale is the killer whale.
Killer whales need to eat lots of food.
They eat seals. Sometimes they even
eat baby blue whales.

Amazing Whale Facts

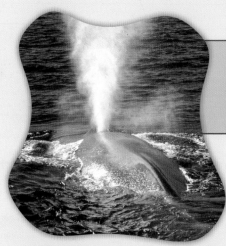

Blue whales blow air up to 6 metres high when they breathe.

Each of a humpback whale's flippers can grow to be as long as a whole dolphin.

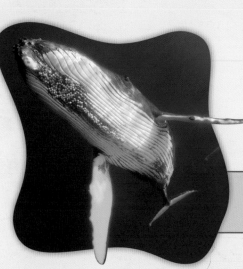

Some whales have small sea animals living on their body.

Sperm whales can dive down about 1,200 metres under the water.

Some whales can live to be 90 years old.

A dolphin can jump 6 metres above the water.

A blue whale calf drinks about 500 litres of milk a day.

Glossary

baleen the part of a baleen whale's mouth that looks like a comb and is used to catch food

blowhole the breathing hole of a whale

calf a baby whale

flippers wide, flat body parts that whales use to swim

mammals animals that are warm-blooded and have hair on their body, that give birth to live babies and feed milk to them

pod a group of whales